Hello.

The You & Me Book

a love journal

Rachel Kempster
Meg Leder

sourcebooks

Published by Sourcebooks, Inc.
P.O. Box 4410, Naperville, Illinois 60567-4410
(630) 961-3900
Fax: (630) 961-2168
www.sourcebooks.com

Library of Congress Cataloging-in-Publication Data

Kempster, Rachel.
  The you and me book : a love journal / Rachel Kempster, Meg Leder.
    p. cm.
  (pbk. : alk. paper) 1. Courtship. 2. Love. 3. Couples. 4. Man-woman relationships. 5. Diaries. I. Leder, Meg. II. Title.
  HQ801.K456 2012
  306.73'4—dc23
                              2012030927

Printed and bound in the United States of America.
VP 10 9 8 7 6 5 4 3

For Michael Bourret and Shana Drehs.

Introduction

YOU KNOW YOUR PARTNER; YOU LOVE YOUR PARTNER!

He favors rocky road ice cream with a heap of sprinkles on top.

She wears the same They Might Be Giants T-shirt and black yoga pants every Saturday.

He's a very safe driver.

Her high school boyfriend rode a Harley.

But we suspect that there's a lot that you don't know. Some silly (what's her favorite junk food?) and some serious (how did your parents meet?). Some happy (where would he love to go on vacation, if money was no object?) and some hopeful (how will you grow older together?).

The You & Me Book will help you answer these questions and more. It's a chance for you, as a couple, to write a book together from start to finish. It's a book that's all about you, your life together, and your hopes and dreams for the future. And the best part? There are absolutely no rules about how you write it! Some couples might finish it over a long weekend; others might spend months passing the book back and forth, answering questions at their leisure. Some prompts might speak to both of you. Others, maybe only one of you will want to explore. Use it however it suits you best.

No matter what your style, we hope that you'll enjoy thinking about the questions, prompts, quotes, and ideas you'll find in *The You & Me Book*. We promise that you will find inspiration on every page—from the wisdom of other couples to the calls to action. When you finish dotting your final "i" on the final page, you and your partner will have found new ways to love each other, new things to laugh about, and new things to consider as you journey through your life together.

XO,

Rachel Kempster
Meg Leder

When you first started dating, how did you keep in touch? Long phone calls? Frequent texting? Facebook messages? Quick emails? Marathon dates? As time has gone on, has that changed or stayed the same? Write about it here.

Describe your first memory of your partner in vivid detail.

Me:

You:

Countless writers, poets, lyricists, and more have documented the craziness of love—the near-mad giddiness you get when you have kick-ass chemistry with someone, the fluttery anticipation you experience when you're getting ready to see them, the single-minded attention you can lavish on someone you love. Document the craziness of your love for each other.

"One is very crazy when in love."

—Sigmund Freud

What couples—both everyday and famous, modern-day and historical—inspire you? What do you wish to emulate from their relationships?

What are you most looking forward to sharing in the future? Why?

How did each of your parents meet? Share the stories with each other, and record the best bits here.

What are the different ways you say "I love you" to each other? List them here. They can be verbal, visual, symbolic, etc.

LOVE ♡ AMARE ♡ AHAVA ♡ LIEBE ♡ AMORE

How did you meet?

At a bar in Wantagh, Long Island! —Tammy O.

We met on a free dating site. His first email to me was asking if I wore Ugg Boots. Personally, I don't care for them, so I responded, "I say no to Uggs." He replied, "Then we can continue to talk." —Courtney M.

Working as teenagers at McDonald's. —Nick C.

We met while I was in college and I was working in a retail store. I was his boss. —Rebecca K.

Through the great and mystical powers of Internet dating. —Michelle T.

We met at a bar in the Hamptons. He asked me if I wanted to dance with his friend, and I said I wanted to dance with him. We couldn't remember what the other looked like over the next two weeks that we talked. We finally went on a real date and the rest is history! —Lauren B.

We met online on a dating website. We met in person six weeks later and canceled our memberships that night. —Kristen G.

He was the intern—what a scandal! —Donya D.

We had mutual friends and met one night cruising around Eighty-Sixth Street in Brooklyn, which was the cool thing to do in the nineties! —Jaimie C.

We met at work. I was working in food service at Skywalker Ranch; Pablo was writing content for the website. We had four lunch outlets, but he came to mine almost every day. I later found out it was because he had a crush on me! —Kristen H.

How did you meet?

My favorite picture of you:

Your favorite picture of me:

While passionate love is made of grand and romantic moments and gestures, everyday love is composed of quiet, regular moments when you're simply *there* for the other person...making chicken soup when he's sick, kissing her with morning breath, etc. List the humble moments that make up your love here.

"Love is not breathlessness, it is not excitement, it is not the promulgation of promises of eternal passion...That is just being 'in love,' which any fool can do. Love itself is what is left over when being in love has burned away, and this is both an art and a fortunate accident."

—Louis de Bernières, *Captain Corelli's Mandolin*

Record your favorite Valentine's Day celebration here. Why is it your favorite?

Spend some time laughing about the bad dates
you had *before* meeting each other.

"The heart is a living museum. In each of its galleries, no matter how narrow or dimly lit, preserved forever like wondrous diatoms, are our moments of loving and being loved."

—Diane Ackerman, *A Natural History of Love*

Create a museum of your relationship. Collect the moments you've loved each other, the moments you've been loved, and record them here.

The author C. S. Lewis wrote, "Friendship is born at that moment when one person says to another, 'What! You too? I thought I was the only one.'" What "You too?" moment have you experienced?

CHECK THEM OFF AS YOU DO THEM!

☐ Gift your partner a silly app.

☐ Wrap a dollar-store present like it's magical and expensive.

☐ Buy him a big bunch of daisies.

☐ Send her a postcard every day for a week.

☐ Buy the ingredients for s'mores, and make them in the microwave.

☐ Get $5 in quarters and hit the arcade.

☐ A pint of ice cream makes a delightful dinner for two, no?

☐ Get big cups of cocoa and go for a long walk in the park.

Chaos theory, the butterfly effect…you've seen it in movies like *Run, Lola, Run* and *Sliding Doors*, the way one small, insignificant moment can ripple out, changing the way your moment, day, and even life develops. Think about how you met. What mutual friend's comment or sliding subway door or stumble on the street led you to each other?

What do you do well together?

What *don't* you do well together?

Getting to Know You: Childhood

Fill in your childhood likes and loves and quirks below.

	YOU	ME
FEAR		
FAVORITE TOY		
BEST FRIEND		
TV SHOW		
HOLIDAY		

	YOU	ME
SCHOOL SUBJECT		
BOOK		
DINNER		
DESSERT		

> "I never understood why Clark Kent was so hell bent on keeping Lois Lane in the dark."
>
> —Audrey Niffenegger, *The Time Traveler's Wife*

What do only you know about your partner? Use this space to share the secret things you know about each other.

> "Deceiving others. That is what the world calls romance."
>
> —Oscar Wilde

We all oversell ourselves a bit on first dates. Is there something in particular you exaggerated? Your fantastic cooking skills (when, in truth, your last three dinners were microwaved) or your love of golf (when you hadn't played since you were 18). When did you finally come clean to each other?

Super You

Draw superhero versions of each other. Play up the things you admire most—amazing parallel parking skills, a love of cats, the ability to kill a centipede in the blink of an eye.

Note: A total lack of artistic talent only makes this more fun!

Super Me

Jane Austen's heroines had piles of love letters to read, reread, and treasure. But modern couples have swapped handwritten missives for texts and emails.

Print out and paste your favorite romantic emails here. Tape them in, fold them up, save them for posterity.

What is love?

It's like when the peanut butter meets the jelly. —Donovan, 11

When somebody likes another person. —Delaney, 7

Someone who kisses you and hugs you. —Matthew, 6

(Shrugs shoulders) I don't know. —Sophie, 4½

It's when you like someone a lot OR they're your family. —Garrett, 3

Love is when you hug someone and your hearts touch. —Neal, 4

Hugs and Kisses, a box of chocolates (in the shape of a heart), and flowers. —Clara, 7¾

Love is Cookie Monster. —Darren, 1½

Love is like when you love some people, like you (mom). I really love my mom. —Jack, 3¾

Love means that I LOVE YOU! —Nate, 5

Love means being together with family. —Jack, 7

Kindness and showing someone what you like about them and how much you care. —Brittan, 9

Love is a feeling that you care about someone and someone cares about you. Like when a couple wants to spend time together and their life together. —Grayson, 7

Love is a sense of joy that somebody brings to your heart. —Haven, 11

Mommy & Daddy. —Jack, 3

What did you think love was when you were a kid?

LIST THE TOP 5 _____ MOMENTS
YOU'VE SHARED AS A COUPLE.

Funniest

1.

2.

3.

4.

5.

Happiest

1.

2.

3.

4.

5.

Vulnerable

1.

2.

3.

4.

5.

Most Romantic

1.

2.

3.

4.

5.

"It is a curious thought, but it is only when you see people looking ridiculous that you realize just how much you love them."

—Agatha Christie, *An Autobiography*

Recall a ridiculous moment—big or small. The time she used salt instead of sugar when making you a pie or the time he surprised you with a night away—only to find he booked a hotel that looked like a potential *Law and Order* crime scene. Record the details here.

JERRY: Which one you wanna go to, schmoopy?
SHEILA: You called me schmoopy. You're a schmoopy.
JERRY: You're a schmoopy!
SHEILA: You're a schmoopy!

—Seinfeld

Use these pages to record your nicknames, silly songs, and other inside jokes you both share.

> "It was an act that came from the same unconscious place that makes a couple, even if they go to bed in a fight, wrap themselves around each other lovingly in their sleep."
>
> —Heidi Julavits, *The Effect of Living Backwards*

Think about the habits you've developed as a couple—the sides of the bed you sleep on, how you drink your coffee in the morning, your going-out routine, how you refer to yourselves as a couple. What things come so naturally to you now that it's as if you've always been together?

Take a class together for something new—making sushi rolls, fly-fishing basics, flower arranging, hot yoga.

Document the experience here.

> "Ultimately the bond of all companionship, whether in marriage or in friendship, is conversation."
>
> —Oscar Wilde

What are your favorite things to talk about with each other?

Does the sight of a cardinal remind you of your bird-nerd mate? Is she crazy for polka dots? Take turns making collages of the colors, images, quotes, memes, and other silly things that remind you of each other. Use magazines, crayons, and anything else fun and colorful that will fill the page.

Write silly haikus for each other. Record the best ones here.
(As you might remember from your school days, a haiku is a three-line poem with
17 syllables in the order of 5-7-5. They're addictive to write once you get on a roll!)

Plan a meal together. Spend time deciding on the menu and drinks, shopping together, and preparing the food. List your menu and drinks here.

"One cannot think well, love well, sleep well, if one has not dined well."

—Virginia Woolf

Record all your firsts as a couple here.

First email:
Date:

Details:

First phone call:
Date:

Details:

First date:
Date:

Details:

First argument:
Date:

Details:

First time meeting each other's friends:

Date:

Details:

First time meeting each other's parents:

Date:

Details:

First gift we gave each other:

Date:

Details:

First vacation we took together:

Date:

Details:

Elizabeth Barrett Browning's famous poem says, "How do I love thee? Let me count the ways." It's your turn. Go on—count them...

Me

You

> "Love makes your soul crawl out from its hiding place."
>
> —Zora Neale Hurston

Fill these pages with your favorite love quotes.

When you first met, what were your dates like? Dinner and a movie? Late-night dive bar hopping? Quiet nights making dinner? Over time, has that changed or stayed the same?

"Love is no earthly power anyhow. It's more like a surrender to a body's pure helplessness. Love is giving up any least little power you ever once had."

—Susan Dodd, *The Mourner's Bench*

What moments in your relationship have made you feel helpless? What have you learned from those experiences?

Getting to Know You: Places

Name your favorites…

	YOU	ME
VACATION SPOT		
PLACE TO RELAX		
FANCY RESTAURANT		
INEXPENSIVE RESTAURANT		

	YOU	ME
CLOTHING STORE		
STATE		
COUNTRY		
PLANET		

When I found out my dad had to do chemotherapy last summer, my boyfriend surprised me the night after I found out by showing up at my apartment door with two dripping cups of gelato and a bouquet of flowers, just to cheer me up. —Mary S.

He told me that our boys are lucky to have me as their mom. —Amy C.

I love how you love me. —Nick C.

Hold a bag for me to get sick in and then give me a kiss. (A peck, he's not gross.) —Kim H.

Letting me be myself—followed closely by saying YES when I proposed. —John G.

She is and has always been one of the most generous people I know. A special gift was when she gave me a locket for our anniversary with a photo of my mom and me inside. It was the summer my mom found out she was dying. —Megan E.

Marrying me. And moving out to Long Island. —Bill M.

WHAT'S THE NICEST THING I'VE EVER DONE FOR YOU?

WHAT'S THE NICEST THING YOU'VE EVER DONE FOR ME?

♥ 65 ♥

If you were to write a romance novel version of your relationship, what would it be like? Fill out the details below.

Title:

Main Characters:

Synopsis:

First Paragraph:

Draw the cover image here:

What physical characteristics did you first admire in each other? Which have you grown to admire over time?

>> >> >> >> >> >> >> >> >> >>

"Tell me more, tell me more
Like does he have a car?"

—Grease, "Summer Nights"

How did you first describe each other to your respective friends? What did you focus on (dreamy brown eyes, a job in IT)? As you've gotten to know each other, has this changed? How?

≫ ≫ ≫ ≫ ≫ ≫ ≫ ≫ ≫ ≫

Alter egos

On *Modern Family*, Phil and Claire have alter egos—Clive Bixby and Julianna—they occasionally use when they go on dates. Same on *Parks and Recreation*: Andy is Bert Macklin, and April is Janet Snakehole.

Create your alter egos. Include history, profession, likes, and dislikes. Then go on a date with each other.

"The course of true love never did run smooth."

—William Shakespeare

Every relationship has bumps in the road. Which ones have you encountered together, and how have you overcome them?

Part of being in love is being there for each other during hard times. Yet it's likely your partner had some tough times before he or she met you. Think of a tough time in your partner's past—whether it was a childhood bullying, a bad breakup, the loss of a beloved pet, or something else. What would you have told your love if you knew him or her back then? Write a letter here.

Found Money

Money is a touchy subject in coupledom—does she think you spend too much? Is he frugal to a fault? Put those practical concerns aside and think about the prompts below. What would you each do if you found a little extra cash? Do you have wildly different answers, or are you like two peas in a pod when it comes to spending?

You find $5 in the street. How do you spend it?

You: **Me:**

Your mom sends $20 in a Halloween card. How do you spend it?

You: **Me:**

You win $100 in the office Oscar pool. How do you spend it?

You: **Me:**

You get an unexpected $1,000 bonus for a job well done. How do you spend it?

You: **Me:**

Tax refund! You're up $5,000 thanks to Uncle Sam. How do you spend it?

You: **Me:**

"So this was how secrets get started, I thought to myself. People constructed them little by little."

—Haruki Murakami, *The Wind-Up Bird Chronicles*

In the space below, record a silly or embarrassing secret you've never shared with each other. Have your partner do the same. When you're done, you can scribble out the secrets together.

MY SECRET:

YOUR SECRET:

What things has your partner taught you about yourself?

ME

YOU

"Love is when you meet someone who tells you something new about yourself."

—Andre Breton

My turn-ons:

My turn-offs:

Your turn-ons:

Your turn-offs:

Our favorite pictures of us together:

"You had me at hello."

—*Jerry Macguire*

Did you fall in love right away, or did it take its time? Write about your path to love here.

Cocktail

Come up with a signature cocktail that celebrates your coupledom. Maybe it's the recipe for the Bloody Mary you made with ketchup and hot sauce in a pinch one snowy Sunday morning? Or something that combines elements of your relationship—sweet Sprite for your cheerful smile, tart grapefruit juice for his sharp wit, and a dash of something stronger to make things interesting?

INGREDIENTS:

List all the books, movies, and songs
that you BOTH love.

List all the books, movies, and songs that you totally don't see eye-to-eye on.

What is "your" song?

Does an entire album count? *The Suburbs* by Arcade Fire was the soundtrack to one of our best weekends together. —Scott S.

"Power of Love" by Celine Dion. —Amy C.

"You Are My Sunshine." —Elissa M.

My husband's nickname is Rio, and when we first dating, he did a wonderful and embarrassing rendition of Duran Duran's "Rio" when we went to karaoke at a dive bar. I have many witnesses, but I wish I had video. —Michelle T.

"Time After Time" by Cyndi Lauper. When we were dating, my roommate walked in on us sitting at the foot of my bed singing it on a karaoke machine. —Kim H.

We have a lot of songs, but probably my two favorites are "Heavenly Day" by Patty Griffin or "For You" by John Denver. —Megan E.

"When I'm 64." —Erin S.

"You Took the Words Right Out of My Mouth," Meatloaf. —Kristen G.

"It Feels Like Home" by Chantel Kresviack. —Nicole G.

"At Last," Etta James. —Beth W.

> "When we die, we will turn into songs, and we will hear each other and remember each other."
>
> —Rob Sheffield, *Love Is a Mix Tape*

Make an old-fashioned mix tape together of songs you both love. List the tracks here for posterity's sake.

SIDE ONE

SIDE TWO

Take a break from the words around you...

...Kiss.

Broken Heart

What lessons have you learned from broken hearts and past relationships? Write down the most significant findings here:

YOU:

ME:

"This is a good sign, having a broken heart. It means we have tried for something."

—Elizabeth Gilbert, *Eat, Pray, Love*

How well do you know each other? Record the responses here and then see how well they match up to reality.

Me

My partner's best friend

My partner's favorite movie

My partner's TV show

My partner's favorite book

My partner's favorite band

My partner's favorite place in the world

My partner's favorite food

My partner's biggest pet peeve

My partner's greatest fear

My partner's favorite color

My partner's favorite season

My partner's favorite time of day

You

My partner's best friend

My partner's favorite movie

My partner's TV show

My partner's favorite book

My partner's favorite band

My partner's favorite place in the world

My partner's favorite food

My partner's biggest pet peeve

My partner's greatest fear

My partner's favorite color

My partner's favorite season

My partner's favorite time of day

Getting to Know You: Favorites

Fill in your favorites below. Where do you agree/disagree most strongly?

	YOU	ME
COLOR		
ICE CREAM FLAVOR		
BEVERAGE		
DAY OF THE WEEK		

	YOU	ME
JOB		
ANIMAL		
OUTFIT		
HOLIDAY		

What familiar tastes, smells, and sounds make up your relationship?

"Maybe this is what love is all about—familiar odors. The taste of someone's skin. The things that fill the senses, not the mind. Not the words a person speaks but the sounds of the words in his mouth surrounded by his voice."

—Maud Casey, *The Shape of Things to Come*

Paparazzi Shot!

Post your best paparazzi shot as a couple here. Were you caught lounging out the beach? All dolled up and sipping martinis at a wedding? Leaving a hot (or not) local restaurant on a sunny Sunday? Now caption it like it's going straight into *Star* magazine.

What's your celebrity couple name? Come up with something even better than Brangelina.

Write a gossip story about your last outing, even if it was incredibly mundane.

Treat Yo Self

On *Parks and Recreation,* Donna and Tom celebrate a tradition called "Treat Yo Self!" One day a year, they treat themselves to things they like—new clothes, mimosas, a massage. However, their colleague Ben has a different wish for "Treat Yo Self" day—and he ends up getting it when he buys a Batman costume.

What does your version of "Treat Yo Self" look like?

YOU:

ME:

TREAT YO SELF!

What does your shared version of "Treat Yo Self" look like?

ME:

YOU:

Now, celebrate!

"Nobody, not even the rain, has such small hands."

—E. E. Cummings

Big brown eyes. A nose full of character. Strong hands. Write a list of your partner's best bits, then share it. Ask your partner to do the same.

"You'll never know everything about anything, especially something you love."

—Julia Child

Are there things your partner doesn't know about you? Not secrets or things that you've purposefully kept tucked away, but little stories from your life that haven't come up yet? Like the Easter when you had a meltdown because the Bunny didn't bring you any Peeps? Or the time you cooked a pot of chili using expired ground beef? Think hard to come up with a few fun anecdotes about yourself that will amuse/intrigue/enlighten your partner. Record them here.

What are the tokens, souvenirs, and mementoes you think best symbolize your relationship? Perhaps it's the first mix tape you made. Or a receipt from the café that served you coffee one good morning. Or a picture of the other person, sent when you were far away. List (or paste) the items here.

> "All you need is love. But a little chocolate now and then doesn't hurt."
>
> —Charles M. Schulz

What foods remind you of your partner? Doodle pictures of your favorite foods together, his favorite foods, and all the foods in between that give you happy memories.

Here's a list of fun, sweet ways you can use technology to amuse and delight your partner.

CHECK THEM OFF AS YOU DO THEM!

☐ Start Pinterest boards for each other with amusing themes. ("*Star Wars* tchotkes I think you'll like" or "Pictures of squirrels wearing tiny clothes.")

☐ Find and collect amusing videos to send to each other on bad days. (Dramatic Chipmunk never gets old—keep that one close at hand.)

☐ Surprise each other with playlists on Spotify.

☐ Send goofy ecards for silly holidays. (National Pickle Day is November 14th, FYI.)

☐ Use instant rim shot whenever possible. www.instantrimshot.com

☐ Create a Google Map to document all your dates, vacations, and favorite places.

☐ Make a Netflix list of the films that make you laugh. Have your partner do the same—then watch them together.

☐ Use faceinthehole.com whenever possible.

☐ Always have two to three games of Words with Friends going. Comment on each other's plays, i.e., "PROEM"? That's not a real word. You cheat!

What are your significant other's favorite activities—the ones he or she loves but does without you? Ultimate Frisbee, knitting, pottery, golf? Try one. Record your impressions here.

>> >> >> >> >> >> >> >> >> >>

LARA: Would it have been lovely if we'd met before?
ZHIVAGO: Before we did? Yes.

—Dr. Zhivago

Do you wish you'd met each other sooner—or was the timing just right? Use the space below to consider what it would have been like if you'd met earlier, or later, in life. What would a shift in time mean for your relationship?

Fill out the following about your partner, and then explain why you chose what you did.

Me:

If you were an animal, you'd be a:

If you were an ice cream flavor, you'd be:

If you were a song, you'd be:

If you were a food, you'd be:

If you were a place, you'd be:

If you were a superhero, you'd be:

If you were a TV character, you'd be:

If you were a(n)_____, you'd be:

You:

If you were an animal, you'd be a:

If you were an ice cream flavor, you'd be:

If you were a song, you'd be:

If you were a food, you'd be:

If you were a place, you'd be:

If you were a superhero, you'd be:

If you were a TV character, you'd be:

If you were a(n)_____, you'd be:

Describe the best day you've ever had as a couple.

First day of our honeymoon in Nice, France. —Simone L.

The first time we said "I love you" is definitely up there, but there was also a pretty wild trip to IKEA in Brooklyn a couple years ago where we saw a woman try to smuggle her dog onto the water taxi and a 10-year-old boy moon a bus full of people in front of the store. —Mary S.

The best days usually involve waking up with coffee and MSNBC, three huge homemade meals, a few hours of instant Netflix, and shopping trips to giant suburban Target and Wegmans. —Tanya R.

Just spending the day on a beach with a deli lunch and getting a time out from parental duties. Felt like we were boyfriend and girlfriend again! —Amy C.

I would say the birth of our daughter, but that did involve a fair amount of pain on my part. So, probably when we drove to Atlantic City when we were dating. We got two flat tires and had to sleep at a rest stop, but that is where we first said we loved each other. —Kim H.

Our wedding day. People are still talking about it over three years later. —Kristen G.

Even though our wedding day was quite the disaster, that is still the best day as a couple. We found the most important things and focused on that and laughed about what had fallen apart. —Courtney M.

In Charles Baxter's *The Feast of Love*, the character Bradley says: "Every relationship has at least one really good day. What I mean is, no matter how sour things go, there's always that day. That day is always in your possession. That's the day you remember...I once talked to a woman who said, 'Yeah, that's the day we had an angel around.'"

What days have you had an angel around?

How has your partner changed your views on the world, in ways big and small? Are you more attuned to the political and social causes he loves? Or perhaps you've become willing to try sushi?

Picnic

Surprise your partner with a spontaneous picnic. Pack the supplies ahead of time—favorite foods, the perfect playlist, a comfy blanket. Find the perfect spot of green grass or just camp out on your living room floor. Record the details here.

A Venn diagram shows relationships in math—you probably remember working with them in junior high. Fill out the Venn diagram of your relationship below. What traits are yours and yours alone? What characteristics, likes, and dislikes do you share?

ME:

US:

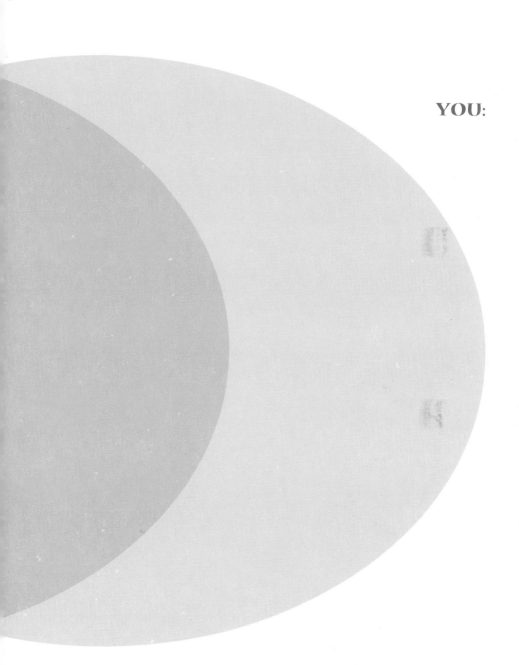

YOU:

Create a series of secret messages for your partner and hide them around the house—in a favorite pair of shoes, a corner of the fridge, under a pillow. Paste them here as you discover them.

With your partner, plan:

A spontaneous day off work

A long weekend

A week's vacation

A monthlong sabbatical

Home Sweet Home

"Our house is a very, very fine house."

—Crosby, Stills, Nash, and Young

Create your dream home together. Where is it? What does it look like?
What makes it yours and yours alone? Sketch it here.

Getting to Know You: Pop Culture

Fill in your pop culture favorites and obsessions below.

	YOU	ME
TV SHOW		
MOVIE		
BOOK		
MAGAZINE		

	YOU	**ME**
ACTRESS		
ACTOR		
SONG		
BAND		
VIDEO		

Books We Want to Read

Restaurants We Want to Try

Places We Want to Visit

Movies We Want to See

Start a TV club. What series have you always wanted to watch but never had the time—*The Wire, Battlestar Galactica, Twin Peaks, The Honeymooners*? List some ideas here, decide on something you both want to watch, and then settle down for some marathon viewing. Record your viewing history here.

Remember the final scene in *The Wedding Singer* when Adam Sandler sings his heart out to Drew Barrymore? Use this space to write a song for your partner that's equally romantic and thrilling and surprising. It can be an entirely original song or a riff on a song that's already been written. ("You are my cupcake, my favorite cupcake" and so on).

(Bonus points for being brave enough to actually sing it to your partner.)

Draw each other. (Feel free to be literal or figurative...whatever works best for you!)

How does your partner make you laugh?

When he plays with our son...he is just another kid! —Tammy O.

He has a terrible knock-knock joke that he tells me whenever I am stressed and overwhelmed. It is an awful joke, but it makes me smile every time, and he knows just when to pull it out. —Rebecca K.

He does "Dancing Man" and I lose it. —Tim C.

When we're in the car and a super cheesy pop song comes on the radio—he busts out some totally ridiculous dance moves. —Michelle T.

Nerdy jokes. —Donya D.

Her comedic timing. —John G.

His comedic timing. —Kristen G.

He has a dry sense of humor I like. He can give me a look in a crowd if something is going on that makes me laugh. —Anne K.

He's really goofy and enthusiastic—which I love. —Erin S.

He makes me laugh by being very nearly the only person in the universe who understands exactly my sense of humor, and we feed off of each other, making ridiculous jokes that spiral out of control and more than likely aggravate those around us. We spend a lot of time alone. —Tanya R.

He makes me laugh by singing ridiculous songs he makes up. —Jaimie C.

He makes me laugh all the time, every single day. That was in our marriage vows "I promise to make you laugh every day." I think he's just the funniest guy ever. —Kristen H.

When he makes fun of my mom. —Lori T.

How do you make each other laugh? Draw, list, and paste in pictures of the things that make you both giggle—from the silly (*Happy Gilmore*) to the sublime (*New Yorker* cartoons about cats).

"Once upon a time there was a boy who loved a girl, and her laughter was a question he wanted to spend his whole life answering."

—Nicole Krauss, *The History of Love*

Write a story together, one sentence at a time. We'll get you started with a classic opening:

Once upon a time...

Surprise!

If you could surprise your partner with anything in the world (money and practicality aside), what would it be? Write about it here, and explain how you made your decision.

ME

YOU

Rescued

How has your partner come to your rescue? Use this space to record and remember the times you needed saving—and how you were saved.

"Where you used to be, there is a hole in the world, which I find myself constantly walking around in the daytime, and falling in at night. I miss you like hell."

—Edna St. Vincent Millay

What do you miss when your partner isn't around? Fill the page with words that describe how you feel when he or she leaves for a minute, a day, or a week.

What are the things that work best in your relationship?

Crushed

There are few things more powerful (and confusing) than a childhood crush. Share the secret details of your youthful loves here. Would you have had crushes on each other back when you were kids? How have your preferences changed over time?

Getting to Know You: Jobs

Who makes the bacon? Who unclogs the drains? Circle your answers below.

Chef   YOU   ME   NEITHER   BOTH

Mechanic   YOU   ME   NEITHER   BOTH

Navigator YOU   ME   NEITHER   BOTH

Shopper   YOU   ME   NEITHER   BOTH

Bartender YOU   ME   NEITHER   BOTH

Driver   YOU   ME   NEITHER   BOTH

Cleaner-upper	YOU	ME	NEITHER	BOTH
Accountant	YOU	ME	NEITHER	BOTH
Dishwasher	YOU	ME	NEITHER	BOTH
Tech support	YOU	ME	NEITHER	BOTH
Bargain hunter	YOU	ME	NEITHER	BOTH
Green thumb	YOU	ME	NEITHER	BOTH

"Find a guy who calls you beautiful instead of hot, who calls you back when you hang up on him, who will lie under the stars and listen to your heartbeat, or will stay awake just to watch you sleep…wait for the boy who kisses your forehead, who wants to show you off to the world when you are in sweats, who holds your hand in front of his friends, who thinks you're just as pretty without makeup on. One who is constantly reminding you of how much he cares and how lucky he is to have you…The one who turns to his friends and says, 'That's her.'"

—Chuck Palahniuk

How does your partner show that he or she feels is lucky to have you?

What do you agree to disagree on?

The musical genius of Amy Winehouse. —Mary S.

Nothing—we both are entirely too stubborn and will pretty much fight our point until the end. But those disagreements are what make life interesting. It usually ends with "so we should probably break up over this?" and then we laugh it off until the next time. —Lauren B.

She loves celebrities; I love politics. I pretend to understand why Beyoncé being pregnant is important, and she pretends to understand why I watch something just to yell at the TV for a few hours. —Scott S.

Where to store the butter. He grew up leaving the stick of butter out in the pantry. I grew up with it in the fridge. We got married and have kept two sticks (one for each of us) ever since. —Amy C.

The date of our first date. —Donya D.

The correct pronunciation of "artichoke." (He says "arty-choke.") —Erin S.

Whether or not vampires should twinkle. —Kristen G.

The pronunciation of the word "dos" as in MS-DOS. —Laurie W.

Social issues. And choices for car colors. —Lori T.

What do you agree to disagree on?

Many people believe there's a difference between romantic love and true intimacy. What do you think they are? How has your partner shown you both?

Me:
Romantic love is:

Examples:

True intimacy is:

Examples:

You:
Romantic love is:

Examples:

True intimacy is:

Examples:

Take pictures of each other modeling different emotions. Make up very specific scenarios. ("I just won the lotto!" "I can't believe *The Sopranos* ended like that!" "Hello lamppost…feeling groovy.") Paste the results here.

"I'll never stop trying. Because when you find the one, you never give up."

—Cal in *Crazy, Stupid, Love*

Do you believe in the idea of a soul mate? Is it just the stuff of movies and sonnets? Write about your belief (or disbelief) of soul mates here.

Me

You

Create a painting together. Start with a blank canvas, and take turns adding and building your own masterpiece. Hang your finished work where you both can see it.

Wishing Well

Here is your wishing well. Write down your wishes for each other.

Best of the Best

Make a list of the best sandwiches (or beer, cupcakes, wine, ice cream, etc.) in your town. Then, make a point of sampling them all together.

MAP OUT YOUR JOURNEY HERE.

Describe your memories of your first kiss together. Was it passionate, awkward, brief, or long? Where did it happen? What was it like?

"The first kiss between two people is something really good in life."

—Juliana Hatfield

"At the first kiss I felt something melt inside me that hurt in an exquisite way. All my longings, all my dreams and sweet anguish, all the secrets that slept deep within me came awake. Everything was transformed and enchanted; everything made sense."

—Hermann Hesse

Collect the ticket stubs and receipts from the movies, meals, and trips to the park you want to remember—paste them here and annotate them for posterity.

Chronicle each other's quirkiest traits, particular habits, intricate likes and dislikes, and charming idiosyncrasies.

ME

YOU

Create online dating profiles for each other—knowing all the quirks, inside jokes, and other silly and serious things you know about each other.

Photo:

Nickname:

Occupation:

Favorite Quote:

Description:

Turn-ons:

Turn-offs:

Photo:

Nickname:

Occupation:

Favorite Quote:

Description:

Turn-ons:

Turn-offs:

Getting to Know You: Vacations

Are you both on the same page when it comes to vacations? Use this quiz to find out where your wanderlust intersects—then start planning a fun trip.

Directions: Circle Y if you'd consider that location for vacation. Circle N if it's completely out of the question.

	YOU		ME	
Hiking Machu Pichu	YES	NO	YES	NO
A beach in Bora Bora	YES	NO	YES	NO
Riding Space Mountain	YES	NO	YES	NO
Vegas, baby!	YES	NO	YES	NO

	YOU		ME	
Leaf peeping in New England	YES	NO	YES	NO
Enjoying meat pies in London	YES	NO	YES	NO
A cruise to Alaska	YES	NO	YES	NO
A tranquil trip to Sedona	YES	NO	YES	NO
Dancing in Miami	YES	NO	YES	NO

Compliment each other

"I like not only to be loved, but also to be told I am loved."

—George Eliot

YOU ROCK! I ADORE YOU! YOU'RE LOVELY!

What are your guilty pleasures as a couple?

Watching as much of certain TV series from Netflix in as little time as possible. —Simone L.

Madonna concerts. —Lance F.

Veronica Mars. Chocolate cake from Amy's Bread. Shake Shack burgers! And cookies. Lots and lots of cookies. —Mary S.

With a bunch of kids, our guilty pleasure is hiring a babysitter and getting out! —Ryan K.

Definitely watching back-to-back episodes of teen dramas such as *Vampire Diaries* and *Skins* (and caring deeply about the people). —Meredith D.

Watching *House Hunters International* episodes on HGTV and eating General Tso's chicken. —Kim H.

An afternoon at Zip's Cafe…great burgers and chicken sandwiches, alongside a few cold beers. Talking to the bartenders and watching football or basketball on TV. —Megan E.

Spoiling our grandchildren, taking vacations. —Anne K.

Homemade fondue. We have it a couple times a year after we put the kids to bed! —Lori T.

We like to eat dinner in on TV trays and watch Jeopardy! —Kristen H.

List your shared guilty pleasures.

Plan the perfect road trip. Below, include a:

* Map of your route
* Songs for the perfect road-trip mix
* Snacks for the perfect road trip
* List of the places you want to see along the way
* List of the people you want to see along the way
* Road trip car questions

"When we get out of the glass bottle of our ego and when we escape like the squirrels in the cage of our personality and get into the forest again, we shall shiver with cold and fright. But things will happen to us so that we don't know ourselves. Cool, unlying life will rush in."

—D. H. Lawrence

Plan a midnight movie drive-in experience for your partner. Select a cult film you both want to watch—*The Goonies*, *Ferris Bueller's Day Off*, *Xanadu*. Buy movie-size candy (Sour Patch Kids and Junior Mints!), make popcorn, grab some blankets, camp out in front of your television, and do a little makin' out. At twelve, hit play.

The movie we watched:

Snacks we ate:

Who stayed awake for the whole thing:

What sides of yourselves do you share with each other and no one else?

What one person do you wish your partner had a chance to meet?

Write each other an old-fashioned love letter. Mail it. (For inspiration, check out Bill Shapiro's *Other People's Love Letters*.)

from:
me
123 main st.
new york, new york
11014

to: the love of my life ♥
456 ferrinill drive
new york, new york
11017

LOVE

How will you grow older together? How do you imagine your lives changing over time? Who will you be ten or twenty years from now?

Congratulations!

You have just completed the über-challenging and exciting task of writing a book—together! You can now officially add "cowriters of *The You & Me Book*" to your relationship credentials—along with partners, best friends, soul mates, etc.

Take time to celebrate: pop open a bottle of champagne and add your autographs to the title page. Find a special place for this one-of-a-kind first edition—the only one like it in the world because it was written by you.

And any time you need to remember the good things in your relationship or to marvel at the love you share or to celebrate the hard work you've put into making your relationship work, consider spending some time with *The You & Me Book*, go through the pages together, revise sections, and add more to your shared story as you write your life together.

Acknowledgments

We'd like to thank:

Michael Bourret, for always being in our corner.

Shana Drehs, for being so enthusiastic and easy to work with, and for taking good care of our books.

The team at Sourcebooks, for designing, selling, and promoting our words.

Megan Mitchell, Steven Leder, Julia Young, and Phoebe Collins for contributing nifty and cool doodles.

Our friends and family, in particular our survey takers, for their generosity and willingness to help us out.

Many, many thanks!

About the Authors

Rachel Kempster works in publishing and lives in Astoria, New York.

Meg Leder is an editor who lives in Brooklyn, New York.

Rachel and Meg are the authors of *The Happy Book* and *The Secret Me Book*.

For more information, visit www.megandrachel.tumblr.com.

Goodbye!